BEAUTIFUL WALL

BEAUTIFUL WALL

POEMS BY

RAY GONZALEZ

American Poets Continuum Series, No. 152

BOA Editions, Ltd. ❖ Rochester, NY ❖ 2015

First Edition
15 16 17 18   7 6 5 4 3 2 1

For information about permission to reuse any material from this book please contact
The Permissions Company at www.permissionscompany.com or e-mail permdude@
eclipse.net.

Publications by BOA Editions, Ltd.—a not-for-profit corporation
under section 501 (c) (3) of the United States Internal Revenue
Code—are made possible with funds from a variety of sources,
including public funds from the New York State Council on the Arts,
a state agency; the Literature Program of the National Endowment
for the Arts; the County of Monroe, NY; the Lannan Foundation
for support of the Lannan Translations Selection Series; the Mary
S. Mulligan Charitable Trust; the Rochester Area Community
Foundation; the Arts & Cultural Council for Greater Rochester;
the Steeple-Jack Fund; the Ames-Amzalak Memorial Trust
in memory of Henry Ames, Semon Amzalak and Dan Amzalak; and contributions
from many individuals nationwide. See Colophon on page 140 for special individual
acknowledgments.

Cover Design: Sandy Knight
Interior Design and Composition: Richard Foerster
Manufacturing: McNaughton & Gunn
BOA Logo: Mirko

Library of Congress Cataloging-in-Publication Data

Gonzalez, Ray.
  [Poems. Selections]
  Beautiful wall : poems / by Ray Gonzalez.
     pages ; cm. — (American poets continuum series ; no. 152)
  ISBN 978-1-938160-83-7 (pbk.) — ISBN 978-1-938160-84-4 (e-book)
  I. Title.
  PS3557.O476A6 2015
  811'.54—dc23
                              2015019653

BOA Editions, Ltd.
250 North Goodman Street, Suite 306
Rochester, NY 14607
www.boaeditions.org
A. Poulin, Jr., Founder (1938–1996)

CONTENTS

Part One

A Judge Orders the Opening of Federico García Lorca's Grave   11
Paul Celan's Ashes   12
Church   13
Gods in the Attic   14
Barrel Cactus   18
Last Night   19
In the Cottonwoods   20
The Mud Angels, Mesilla, New Mexico   21
Las Brujas de La Mesa, New Mexico   28
Hummingbird on the Porch   29
Double Seasons   30
The Fields of La Mesilla   31
Antlers in the Tree, Livermore, Colorado   33
Teacher   34
Stone Cushion   35
Axis   36
They Call the Mountain Carlos   37
The Border Is a Line   38
One El Paso, Two El Paso   40
Landscape Is an Abstraction   42
Sticky Monkey Flowers, Monterey Bay   44

Part Two

Julio Cortázar's Cat   47
Again   49
Give History a Chance   51
Driving Past a Missile Silo Near Langsden, North Dakota   53
The Lynching Postcard, Duluth, Minnesota   54
Fucking Aztecs, Palomas, Mexico   55
Burning Breast   57
Touch   58
Stone   59
The Donkey Cart Apparition, Las Truchas, New Mexico   60

Meditation at Canutillo — 61
Lies — 64
Crossing New Mexico with Weldon Kees — 67
Snow Fields on Fire — 73
To Be — 75
The Sacred Fire — 76
Cadets at the Virginia Military Institute Read *Howl and Other Poems* by Allen Ginsberg — 78
The War Museum — 79
The Destroyer of Compasses — 81
My Nephew's Army Helmet — 83

Part Three

Three Unfinished Masterpieces — 87
Max Ernst with His Collection of Kachinas, New York, 1936 — 88
René Char Paints on a Piece of Bark During a Night of Insomnia — 89
The Soul Can't Paint Itself — 90
Bald Eagle North of Shelby, Montana — 91
The Plain of Hooves — 93
The Drums — 94
Hospital — 95
Nicanor Parra — 97
Violins — 98
17-Year-Old Robert Zimmerman Attends a Buddy Holly Concert in Duluth, Minnesota, January 31, 1959 — 99
Bob Dylan's Newport Guitar — 100
Duane Allman with the Cross — 103
Captain Beefheart Leaves His Body — 104
Invisible Guitar — 105
Driving Around El Paso, Marvin Gaye's "What's Going On" Comes on the Radio — 106
Zodiacal Light — 108
The Face of the Sun — 110
Hair — 111
Max Jacob's Leather Coat and the Possibility of Grief — 113
Jack Kerouac Brings His Mother to the Mexican Border, 1957 — 114

Satellite   120
Two Hawk Skies in Minnesota   121
The Edge of the Wilderness, Northern Colorado   123
The Dance   125
I Once Knew the Black Rider   126
Hunchback   127
A Period of Ashes   128
The Theory and Practice of Love   129
The Riches   130

Acknowledgments   *132*
About the Author   *134*
Colophon   *140*

Part One

A JUDGE ORDERS THE OPENING
OF FEDERICO GARCÍA LORCA'S GRAVE

Leave the dead alone.
Federico is not with the other eighteen bodies that were dumped there.

Do not rewrite the myth.
Federico is not there because his poem about

the moon lifted him away long ago.
No poet leaves bones as clues to where they must go.

Do not open the earth.
Federico emerged long ago and hid among the black trees

to get away from the death song, the others slowly moving
to the sound of his footsteps, their bodies stripped of possessions,

though the murderers left a folded piece of paper in Federico's pants.
Do not unfold it and read what they did not read because Federico

took the words off the bloody page and ran.
He is gone and will not greet the shovels because your law is not

for tracing the saint. It is for entombing the written word,
but you will discover that poetry is not buried down there.

PAUL CELAN'S ASHES

Here is the hand in its shade of absolute
and the study of grapes with bruises.

If the river took the body,
how did it burn?

Here are constellations stained in the books,
the sentence hidden from the truth,

executions painted on the sun
as if what is here must be understood.

If black hands reach for the sun,
how do ashes mask the face of history?

Here is the measure of the body, the rain
that drips on what has been done—

a greater telling vague with tongues.
If stepping into the void is a cut flower,

how does war leave survivors?
Here is the healing hand on the throat,

the good heart and its water spilled
when things are finally understood.

If the poem takes the soul,
how does sound embrace it?

If this is silence,
how does the bird bend the tree?

CHURCH

When the old women approached the church,
they knelt on the concrete, penance to their Lord
about to be paid as they slowly moved toward
the doors on their knees, one woman in tears,
the other muttering in silence, each one granted
something from the one they believed, paying
back on their burning knees, their heads draped
in scarves, summer dripping on the hot concrete
as they awkwardly moved toward the doors,
church goers stepping out of their way
as they approached the arch, standing back
because they did not have the same need,
did not ask for what could never be granted
as they stared at the two women approaching
the entrance this way, each one pausing
down there to make the sign of the cross,
stopping as people around them dipped fingers
in the dirty cups mounted on the wall, blessing
themselves before getting out of the way,
the silent women unable to reach the holder
of holy water, refusing to stand up and insert
their fingers as others did, their scorched knees
keeping them in the entryway, people going
around them as the two women let out moans
and prayers, a small boy appearing out of
the arriving crowd, pausing behind the kneeling
women to tap the holy water with his small
fingers, sprinkling drops on the backs of
each kneeling woman, then crossing himself
before his parents grabbed him and pushed
him into the cool darkness of the church.

GODS IN THE ATTIC

1.

Cardboard box in my grandfather's
house, old man starving his kids,
my father shining shoes on street
corners at the age of five,
the old man dying thirty years ago,
my rare visit allowed while others
are gone, the stairs to the attic as
dark as the reasons to keep away.

No movement from cobwebs,
box I rip open to find art prints
of Aztec gods, descriptions of each
at the bottom reminding me I was
taught pyramids are for destruction,
not for getting to the other world.
Someone saved these drawings
to keep me climbing the stairs.

2. Huehuecoyotl

God of music flying over the flames
of the mother, drum beating until
his heart falls in a river of feathers,
a light with black diamonds tossed
to the warriors who impregnate
their women—Huehuecoyotl
releases the flowers because men
born in this fertile period grow to
be singers and storytellers,

Huehuecoyotl tossing colors as
fragrant as the night, the priests
claiming sons of the flower period
would become overindulgent
at the waterfall where the storyteller
dove and was not seen again until
someone wrote the truth.

Two-headed figure of a man and coyote—
his power too alien for the text
I have been writing for fifty years.
When I set the print down,
I hear a rustling in the corner,
dim light destroying what floats
in the air.

3. Ilamatecuhtli

Goddess of the earth, death,
and the Milky Way greets me
with her spread legs, though
the sun breached her universe
before I came along.
She is an aged woman with
fleshless mouth, large bared
teeth and dressed in white.
Ilamatecuhtli holds a shield
and baton and I have seen
this woman in white before,

known her in the story of
the river, why her temple was
known as "darkness" when
the locked ward of the mental
hospital kept me for days,
women in white wearing her

seashells to tease me into getting
well, the room making me doodle
drawings of faces while I waited.

Ilamatecuhtli appears in star skirt
and the attic door closes, my trouble
breathing making me set her down,
the woman in white pointing to
constellations Sagittarius and Auriga.
I pick up the drawing and she brushes
my face with the poem of healing.

4. Itzamna

God of writing wrinkled in the closet.
Itzamna brings his screenfold book
and drops it in my aching lap, his
second role as a healer surprising me
because I want to close the box and
run away, my desire to fold
the prints quickly passing and I open
the roll to allow Itzamna to walk
to his writing stone, symbols revealing
the lizard—reptile I knew as a child,
the white lizards of my recurring dream
snowing on the picture of the writer
kneeling over his stone.

5. Xochipilli

His vision is folding the sun into
the secrets of my father's family
that never allowed me to know them,
their silence clashing with Xochipilli,
another patron of scribes, the last print

of the codex he created made
of hundreds of my failed poems,
old paper thrown away, weak lines
I have laughed at, rejecting their
unconvincing shadows, a cycle
that demands I see what I should
have faced long ago, ceremonies
no one will ever witness because
Xochipilli traces a symbol that
is mine alone.

Movement downstairs, so I put
the prints away, push the box into
the corner, its torn lid falling over
newspapers that discolor the art
of hidden beliefs, though these
prints are for decoration and not
for those whose faith was
sacrificed at the altar long ago.

BARREL CACTUS

In the 1932 photo, my grandmother Julia
and her sister pose in front of a huge barrel

cactus, the round plant reaching their waists as
they stand behind it and squint into the camera,

the enormous barrel of water wider than
the two women together, who will serve their

husbands in the Arizona desert, have children,
and be punished for drinking from the well.

Julia's polka-dotted dress reaches the ground,
while her sister's white skirt and coat add to

the white hat she wears, the light from it
reflecting beyond the barrel covered with

thorns that grow down the sides, barbs the women
would love to wear if they found a way to open

the giant barrel and decorate themselves with
what naturally comes weeping from the earth.

LAST NIGHT

Last night, the bees came, the tops
of the barrel cactus split open
by the heat, bees darting into the night
to find the place they belonged.
I heard them in the canyon and waited
inside the broken trunk of the cottonwood,
hiding in there to learn how swarms of bees
hum about the future in their sleep,
so sweet desert soil remains and is no
longer the honey that sticks to my lips,
opening the dirt road until I find
the slashed barrels and take a drink.

Last night, the bats followed their flight
out of Carlsbad Caverns to feed on peyote
plants that grow around the entrance,
this well-documented myth broken when
I reached the opening in the earth and saw
the blue lights, headed back to my car
because I approached the wrong cave,
smelled the smoke, bats brushing my head
with the smell of guano that made me
leave without entering the ground.

Last night, a mountain lion wandered into
the town and was trapped in a car wash,
police shooting it, the streets marked with
the claws of the old, my hands slapping walls
and leaving a mark, a distant hum mistaken
for light poles blinking across the city,
the clay jars on my porch brimming with
water where bees hovered until I went into
the great fields of cactus, waving to the river
to follow me without flooding the earth.

IN THE COTTONWOODS

Often in the cottonwoods, I used
to see a man walk like a spirit,
thought he could be my lost uncle,
missing for fifty-two years, or the kneeling
woman who said there was nothing
moving behind the rows of candles
and it was okay to lift my head.
I heard a voice call across the river
without looking for me in those twisted
branches and hidden leaves.

When I moved closer, I startled
a sleeping dove, its wings taking
me to its hidden nest where
I saw what I had never seen—strings
of light giving birth to the tiniest
things that sent me away,
heavy limbs bristling in shadows
that punished me by revealing
where candles truly flame.

Now, I rarely go into those trees
with justice and search for
bark peeling off the branches.
So often in the cottonwoods,
I saw a man standing like a rumor
forgotten in the wind.
The final time, I was sure it was him,
but all I found rooted there were my
hands and the rhythm of those trees.

THE MUD ANGELS, MESILLA, NEW MEXICO

after Rafael Alberti's Concerning the Angels

The Unknown Angel

I cannot sleep because the mud angel
enters the new century through the dirt streets,
spreads his wings on the mud walls of yesterday,
freezing himself in place so boys can lean
against the adobe and weep for the passing years
of asking for something to believe.

I cannot sleep because the ashes outside
the window rise like the angel that plastered
these walls in the illumination of tomorrow,
the river drying into mud angels that spread
their arms each time someone is killed
on the other side.

I cannot sleep because the figure remains
unnamed, streaks of fresh mud decorating
the timbers on the ceiling as if a circle of wings
is the nest of grief, the good angel whirling
faster to finish plastering the walls, morning
light marking the fact there are no doors.

The Angel of Numbers

The angel of numbers waits in the puddles
left after the war, hungry boys refusing to add
their fingers together, cries from these adobe

houses echoing in fires where the women
wait to teach the potted cactus how to count
each other because everyone has fled these

walls, the mathematician of mud crossing
and recrossing the numbers, until the abandoned
houses add up and these dirt streets equal

what one boy possesses—muddy hands that streak
and change his numbers on the walls allowing
him to sleep in that room.

Song of the Luckless Angel

Are you obsessed with the mud of yesterday?
Who constructed the bricks and who gave
you a chance to enclose yourself within?

Look at me.
I am covered in mud and no one will place
a street sign where paradise ends because

I am here, buried under the graves of ancestors
who cooked in the mud ovens, gave birth on
the mud floors, even ate this dirt that gave me wings.

Are you obsessed with the rain of tomorrow?
When it washes me away, I will show you
how the streets of Mesilla remember.

Tell me who I am.

The Undecided Angel

When the mud angel could not decide
which street to bless, the gates of the town

shut and the arches of heaven disintegrated
into fine dust because what comes from

the muddy earth rises over these streets,
ideas as rare as the wings brushing the roof,

sounding as if someone is going
to come in and touch your face.

When the angel could not decide
how to get away, the gleaming mud

ornamented what he could not take
with him, the beauty of theft drying

into the shape of a mud foot that
does not wear the feathers

to leave a mark at the first door,
someone waking to convince himself

there is a confused angel and it
keeps leaving his earthly dreams.

The Enraged Angel

I move down Palacio Street and
the windows on the mud apartments
remain closed, their drapes dripping
into fine shapes that color the sidewalk,
the western sky burning as if wings
were outlawed and the angry man
cannot become the angel that protects
each figure that crosses the street.

I move down San Cristobal and see
the empty well, the house of the *espanto*
refusing to burn, the mud shaping itself
as if no one owns it, the anger of the

wingless man becoming the daily waking
cry of the one who ascended through
the broken roof to warn the rest of us
that to walk on the morning streets
is to witness the rising of the enraged
angel who will no longer hide here.

I move down a nameless road
and refuse to believe it,
cross the empty corral until
a rustling makes me stop.
"Who are you?" someone asks.

The Charcoal Angel

Charcoal and mud,
the black vein of gold.
Wings and broken shapes.
History of walls and whispers
forced to have faith in the cross
of outspread arms.

When I found the charcoal angel,
he was drawn on the longest wall,
his face crisscrossed by thorns left
behind when conquest was still a game.

When I traced the charcoal angel,
he tried to move out of my reach,
his enormous wings not even looking
like wings—those arms and clouds
a joke in the confessions of small things.

When I found the charcoal angel,
he shifted his weight and the wall cracked,
the prayer I forgot when I was old

returning as if the flakes on the wall
were made to be held to my lips,
the taste of the earth the bitterness
of those who keep alighting here.

The Angel of Walls

I came to the wall,
ancient barrier whose builder
left on a secret road.
I touched the disintegrating bricks
in search of the missing revolution,
quilted steps of mud returning
the ground to its freedom.
I pushed against the dusty height,
wanting to hear the cry of things,
my thirst reaching for the well in the yard.

I came to the wall and felt
the guilt of its silence,
recalled a pair of white hands
painted in a corner long ago,
their image rising on a morning
of fear, then washed in rains
that pushed the roof in.
Out of the adobe came a dark
figure singing of the morning.
It was I in another time where
I built these walls to stay.

I walked under the arches,
waited for hands to mark
the opening in the earth,
my actions forgiven when I found
no escape, only the smell of goat
meat frying in the dark and open land.

I entered the room of the sun,
was blinded by holes exploding
in the walls, flowers of light hiding
their destination, a spot on the floor
where someone rose and whispered
long ago, "I remember."

I stood by the wall where promises
were made before the cracks led to
the reaches of sleep, geometry working
to the straw heaped in each corner,
threads from the other house where
the maker lived with brown hands,
his ovens glowing in early evening.

I touched the wall and went beyond it,
tasting grains of dirt on my tongue
as I emerged through the hole behind
the altar erected centuries ago, then
stepped outside to follow footprints in
the dirt leading to the next wall.

The Angel of Mystery

What if I said it was thick mud
up to my elbows?
What if I showed you it was
red mud bristling with arrows?
What if the mud mask did not
have wings?
Who would believe me and
who would say it is a sin?

When the mud angels looked like
the old ones I wanted to be,
I was too young to be taken with mud.

When the priest burned his mission down,
eighteen angels were found under the floor.
When the humidity of oblivion named
this place Mesilla, I was born.

LAS BRUJAS DE LA MESA, NEW MEXICO

They hide in the pueblo, suffering inside
the adobe walls, waiting for the trees

to pierce the wooden heart of the last
child that was found alive.

Las brujas de La Mesa wait for us to enter
as if our mothers' wombs were holy.

They hope we turn the car to the river where
they mix bones with blood of the lizard,

spit into a bowl to find a bruised eye.
If we get out of the car, the road will end at

La Mesa, but the road never stops because
we saw a woman behind a tree, her words

in charcoal as black as the hands that pulled
us into the empty town.

Las brujas bless the wind with chicken feathers,
smother the room we dare not enter because

they slip through windows to braid the hair
of the dead we read about in books, one house

crumbling with no roof, the woman who lives
there drifting among us since the invisible

have no shadow, torches glowing in the street
that night as we leave without a sign, twisted

trees patterned after the things all men
are forced to leave behind.

HUMMINGBIRD ON THE PORCH

Suddenly, it hovered a couple of feet
in front of my face, tiny black head

on white body buzzing like a god
choosing to accept me, seconds going by

as the hummingbird floated there,
close to my face, the air of its wings

brushing me as if I finally deserved it.

DOUBLE SEASONS

These are the double seasons of loss, the horizon
where red mountains are old sunsets, the empty truck

swirling down the dirt road, heavy with outlawed cargo.
These are the days of ceremony and holy thoughts,

communion in abandoned churches where horses
and men were destroyed long ago, a legend still untold.

There are two tracks in the sand, one leading north
and one disappearing at the razor wire, graffiti

running down the locked doors, the sound of a lone
whistle shattering the air with the cry to go.

These are guesses and the eternal wish for time,
other desires painting forests on ocean floors.

These are the months of difference,
the begging women chipping away at houses,

hands gripping windows to rescue the dead as they
ask for a prayer without exposing one breast or feeding

the starving dog dropping on the black porch.
These are the double seasons of love and cut flowers,

pollen covering statues of the unknown, buried
family breathing the dusty wind and sleeping as if

two growing seasons, minus the harvests,
are enough to love the earth at any cost.

THE FIELDS OF LA MESILLA

There are no adobe arches to stand under.
They have melted in the rain.
This is not about mud, but the way
the sun changes everything.
Even the field of earthly blood
crumbles in labor to itself.
God named it and took away the harvest.
It is not wisdom or loss,
merely the path to the bridge where
no one crosses the river anymore.
There are no flags or ribbons
to hide in antique cabinets.
They have been set out and there
is a silence behind the doors.
The horizon wants something more,
but the fields celebrate the evening light
under the mountains that rise and close.
On one of those nights, a man sits up
in the dark and lights a candle or two.
No one trusts him and no one cares
his sons are gone, the tools of yesterday
rusting in the dirt where their mother
was last seen shaking an old rag doll.

There are no adobe arches to deface.
They have been torn down in the heat.
This is not about miracles, but of the animal
that leaves the water in its stillness.
Its tracks spell faith in the hunt and things
that spoil underground—acres of cotton
and vegetables steady in the shade.
Old pickup trucks circle in the dust.
There is a ritual of hot chile and shouts
that must be performed, the fields

turning brown because no one is hungry,
fewer are afraid, and the man with candles
is the man to be loved because when
the arches smell like cottonwood,
it is a night when La Mesilla moon
glows above the valley and, behind its sphere,
there are many empty rooms.

ANTLERS IN THE TREE, LIVERMORE, COLORADO

The Poudre River called me south,
so I removed my horns and stuck
them high in the tree by the dirt road.
If you can't believe this and laugh,
then I admit I saw an animal rub
itself against the trunk, shedding
its horns to brighten the branches.
I really wasn't there, but want to
claim a place under the shade of a tree
decorated with horns, bone branches
that belong there so we can look up
and dream we truly know.

Perhaps, the horns have been lodged
for too long, and might become
an extension of limbs the tree
was missing when the animal stopped
there, grazed for a second, then entered
the tree for the last time, pushing
and pulling, stomping its hoofs
until the locked horns gave way.
The river called me south and I pulled
two antlers from the highest fork, never
looked back because other horns are
embedded there, points from a stillness
sharper than the changing tree.

TEACHER

for Robert Burlingame, 1925–2011

He stood under the old cottonwood
and held some of its leaves in his hands.

"Each word is right here," he said.
"They are written down, one word per leaf."

I studied one yellow leaf and saw nothing
except the brittle yellow before he took it

from me and crushed it crisply in his hand,
dropping the gold dust in the dirt.

The huge tree had shadowed us for decades.
We used to read poems there, but the Rio Grande

shifted course over the years, began flowing
like a tired woman as it now passed the tree

near our favorite spot, its water turning blue
the instant he crushed the leaf.

STONE CUSHION

Translation brings a light so
divine, you are embarrassed.

When one praises, one demands
a great secret in return.

The walk down the mountain was
easy, though there was an empty cup

and a mortician full of joy.
This time of year there is a celebration

where you preserve a clay jar decorated
with the king Arzltkohaklytl's face.

You could close your eyes and instill
the soil to dig up its monolith, though it

would create faith in what would come
later and napalm has kissed that spot.

What if the question was a hard cushion
where the emperor sat to survive?

He could smoke sitting there because
his language will be crushed by cathedrals.

AXIS

The volcano in my grandmother's Mexican village
smothered the town, though the girl escaped because
the axis of revolution sent her family into exile,

black clouds covering their journey to the north.
The axis of the earth is a skeletal bone extending
from pole to pole, the arm of someone holding on.

The Japanese earthquake shifted the axis of the earth,
moving Japan twelve feet closer to North America,
each day shortened by one second.

When a poet said the past never happens because
it is always present, the other one proclaimed the past
is in the future, the axis bending to allow these words

to skip the water like stones thrown by a boy in
search of his father, the axis of yesterday sinking
the stones the boy hurled across the pond.

THEY CALL THE MOUNTAIN CARLOS

They call the mountain Carlos because
it is brown, though its purple slopes
at dusk suggest other names.
Those who name it have to brand
the earth with something they know—

a name, a face, even the heat that says
"I know Carlos and he is the mountain.
I am going to cover his eyes in light."
They call its peak Carlos because
it is the sharpest feature on the face
that stares south, watching people
cross the border, pausing to catch
their breath and meet the cliffs of
Carlos because he is there.

When they ascend the canyons inside
the face, Carlos shifts and the climbers
discover what he has done.
The moving earth changes everything
and they are forced to stop playing
the game of naming a mountain
that keeps touching the sun.

THE BORDER IS A LINE

The Mexican border is a line between
faith and the shackled dream.

When people cross it, the highways
lead north and west.

When they are stopped and taken,
the green vans go south.

The border is a line between
imagination and the truth—

those who make it will not return,
the line leading to bodies in lost graves.

The line extends from birth to death,
though the mountains get in the way,

the line curving around them
to gather strength.

The line becomes a long sentence
when the labor matters, survivors

straightening the line to align it
with the relentless sun, stars falling

above the hole where they hide.
Even the bloodline from a plastic

bottle of water to a picture of La Virgen
de Guadalupe is sacrificed at the wire

because the Mexican border is a line
between faith and its sharpest point—

a line that is infinite, unstoppable,
and is coming this way.

ONE EL PASO, TWO EL PASO

Awake in the desert to the sound of calling.
Must be the mountain, I thought.

The violent border, I assumed, though the boundary
line between the living and the dead was erased years ago.

Awake in the sand, I feared, old shoes decorated with
razor wire, a heaven of light on the peaks.

Must be time to get up, I assumed. Parked outside,
Border Patrol vehicles, I had to choose.

Awake to follow immigration shadows vanishing inside
American walls, river drownings counted as they cross,

Maria Salinas' body dragged out, her mud costume
pasted with plastic bottles and crushed beer cans,

black water flowing to bless her in her sleep.
Must be the roar of illegal death, I decided,

a way out of the current, though satellite maps never
show the brown veins of the concrete channel.

Awake in the arroyo of a mushroom cloud, I choke,
1945 explosion in the sand, eternal radioactive wind,

the end of one war mutating the border into another
that also requires fatal skills of young men because few

dream the atomic bomb gave birth in the Jornado,
historic trail behind the mountain realigned, then cut

off from El Paso, the town surrounded with barbed
wire, the new century kissing car bombs, drug cartels,

massacres across the river, hundreds shot in ambushes
and neighborhood soccer games that always score.

Wake up, I thought, look south to the last cathedral
in Juarez before its exploding bricks hurtle this way.

Make the sign of the cross, open your eyes to one town,
two cities, five centuries of praying in the beautiful dust.

LANDSCAPE IS AN ABSTRACTION

The Rio Grande empties into the Gulf
of Mexico where Cabeza de Baca crossed
Texas, following the blue smoke of the shaman
toward the mountains of the healing root.
I emerged at San Cristobal, red cliffs nearby,
the last fence fallen, dirty fires behind my back.
A hawk I spotted kept the sun alive, vanished
when the coyote on the hill ran backwards.
Don Juan de Onate fell off his horse forty miles
north of El Paso del Norte, his leg swollen
when the Spanish expedition finally crossed
El Jornado del Muerto, purple mountains
ending at the river as if it was never there.

When one of their dogs disappeared in
a canyon, the conquistadores never found
it, named the place Perro Perdido, fields
of yucca and rock leading to the walls
where hands of the people marked souls
and insisted this is the way to go.
I crossed Dos Avilas behind the plateau,
found the path to the ancient stone lions
as clear as the line between here and
the cross atop the rusting tower at
Lookout Point, sheer rock above and
below, the marked stones resembling
fallen horses, perhaps a horned creature
never seen but eternally known.

Kit Carson attacked the Kiowas and
his army killed women and children,
the marker on the ridge at Sangre de Oro
leading me there, thick pines blocking
my view, the sound of an animal nearby

breathing into the matted floor of needles.
I found water and the rustling of birds,
the mask worn by San Simón removed
when he reached the well.

The tree stump in the Valley of Fires was
surrounded by lava, Little Black Peak
the last place I saw a dark figure move,
the stump the same I found decades ago.
The figure's cape rose as he pointed
northwest toward Carrizozo.
I placed my hands on the trunk and
it erupted in a rush of wasps.

When rebellious people in the pueblos
killed the Spanish, the friars fled south,
the river waiting in blood, ox carts
loaded to break down in a desert
unmarked to this day, the point
of turning back proving one wagon
wheel becomes two suns rising and
falling, cliffs eroding with Trinity Site
nearby, whitewashed and radiant
ground the place to step across
the white sand, ocotillo bushes
and Spanish daggers steaming in
the lava fields of yesterday.

STICKY MONKEY FLOWERS, MONTEREY BAY

When flight kept track of the line of pelicans,
there was a roar across the bay, distant white specks

in the sky vanishing like the seeds of nourishment,
cold pardons combining infinite movement

with the words for the kindest news of water.
Sticky monkey flowers spreading into sunlit nerves,

moving in the mist like a distant yellow horizon
taking its time coming back.

Blossoms lifting, small and untroubled,
given their green moisture to fill the eye after

the fever breaks, after sand drifts into hidden coves
of disaster, one lone pelican making it back in time

to avoid the shape moving across the plants that
twist sand with wind, flower scent with muscle,

as they leave the unknown out of the garden,
the unspoken out of the drifts of what has been.

Part Two

JULIO CORTÁZAR'S CAT

It came to me the other night
and I woke to find my two cats
also waiting for Theodor Adorno.
They sat at the foot of my bed
and peered into the darkness,
did not react to a third animal
invading their territory, but purred.

I sat up and knew it was Cortázar's cat.
It circled my bed twenty-five years after his death.
Theodor Adorno was alive and had
appeared in a number of his books
before joining my cats.

Cortázar wrote that his black cat gazed
into the void and brought things that
were needed so its owner could write.
He claimed his cat was the master of the Tao,
the spirit needed for a purer life.
He compared Adorno's power to the hole
Navajo women leave in their ponchos to
not suffocate the soul imprisoned inside.

Suddenly, I realized where I had
failed and jumped out of bed.
This startled my cats and they ran
into the kitchen as Adorno leaped
onto the window sill.
I raised it and Cortázar's cat leaped out
and ran across the yard, its shadow
crossing in an early light.

I closed the window and went into
the kitchen, but couldn't find my cats.

They vanished for two days, then
reappeared at the foot of my bed
on a night I could not sleep.
I stared at the darkness as their
sudden purring covered my head.

AGAIN

after Evan Connell

Olmecs from the Mesoamerican civilization created
ceramic figurines of dogs running on wheels tied

to their feet by wooden axles, similar to those found
in Mesopotamian tombs.

It is believed the skill of a water diviner comes from an
area in the elbow whose veins connect to the paranormal.

I was afraid so I sat down, again.
The dirt was warm, but it was there.

A dove was seen flying from Joan of Arc's mouth a few
seconds before she was killed, though you can't find

a bare female foot in Chinese art because its artists can
depict nakedness, but cannot touch the female foot.

I was concerned so I rose to my knees.
The dirt had crude lines drawn into it.

It has been determined that the Church does not
take any action against a priest who has gone mad.

A Roman tombstone near Antibes tells of a twelve-year-old visitor
from the North who danced and gave pleasure to many.

I didn't understand, so I rose to my feet, again.
The dirt turned to glass and I thought I could see.

When the first Europeans arrived in the Aztec nation,
its people were already revolting against repression,

bands of them arming themselves for war and sacrifice,
willing to help the invaders burn the city down.

The pacifist Mohandas Gandhi's corpse was
transported to his funeral on a gun carriage.

I finally saw what it was and followed the trail.
The walls crumbled and I left my handwriting there.

GIVE HISTORY A CHANCE

When Hernán Cortés burned Mexico City,
the lake rose to the level of his crucified god,
the Aztec aviaries releasing thousands
of birds in the smoke.

When Coronado's men got lost going
north along the Rio Grande, their horses
drowned one by one, each man swimming
toward a cross of light.

When the defenders of the Alamo tried
to escape without putting up a fight, sixty
of them were killed by the Mexicans one
hundred yards outside the walls, revisionist
history giving them a chance to run.

When morning came and Pancho Villa
was shot twenty-four times in his car, two small
children stood at the street corner,
bullets flying over their heads, their
mother screaming at them to get inside.

When the drug cartel gunned down
fourteen soccer players in the Juarez field,
the masked shooters were driven to
a safe house where every wall was
covered in shrines to San Malverde,
their patron saint shot by police in 1903.

As the killers pulled their masks off
and laid their weapons down, sweat
glistened across their tattooed backs,
the young, panting men kneeling
to kiss the concrete floor in front

of the mustached saint, their cell
phones starting to ring, their red faces
shining like the blood of Mexico City
the birds abandoned before reforming
in the black skies over the lake.

DRIVING PAST A MISSILE SILO
NEAR LANGSDEN, NORTH DAKOTA

Twenty miles south of the Canadian border,
the missile would rise across the high plains

and fuse north over the Arctic toward Russia.
It must have been the plan because the lone jeep

with two soldiers sits by the gate, watching
rare traffic pass on the two-lane country road,

the barbed-wire fence surrounding
the bunker as if something might escape.

In Langsden, there is a friend's wedding
next to a grade school where a huge replica

of a missile towers on the playground,
the warhead its mascot, the white erection

lifting over kids who might dream of
getting out of there someday.

Leaving the ceremony, the road points south
and the jeep is gone on the way home,

the concrete and fence bristling with antennas
that slash the hills and the low canyons,

the underground system rusting and ready,
vast fields of wheat and sugar beets needing

to be harvested before the white sun
appears and ruins everything.

THE LYNCHING POSTCARD, DULUTH, MINNESOTA

There is a postcard in an antique shop in Duluth
with a photograph of the infamous lynching of
a black man carried out in the town in the 1930s.

The owner was turned down by eBay when
he wanted to sell it there. Tourists walk into
his shop and stare at the lone card in the glass case.

The owner says it is better to sell it
than donate it to a museum where
it would be locked away in a drawer.

Some people want it removed.
Others snicker and stare, shake their heads
and accept the fact this is "only Minnesota."

Each morning, the shop owner glances
at the case to make sure the postcard is there.
Thousands have bowed over the glass.

At night, when the shop is closed,
the postcard lies in the case, the body hanging
in the cold moonlight from Lake Superior,

the shadow from the swinging body
forming a shape that rises through
the glass to darken the shop.

Over a dozen people have come across it.
They don't know the act of bending over the glass
to study the dead body on the pole is forming

an invisible arc of light over time,
a shadow where those who bow to look
imitate the shape of a hanging tree.

FUCKING AZTECS, PALOMAS, MEXICO

Small clay figurines on a market shelf—
eight couples entangled in different positions,

Aztec men kneeling, mouths wide open,
giving it from behind, one woman standing

on her head, thighs spread as her mate
slides it in from above.

The sculptor who molded the huge cocks
laughs in an alley house somewhere in Palomas

because the statues don't sell, *turistas* walking
by the display window without noticing because

the Aztecs sit on the highest shelf, my curiosity
spotting them by chance as I drew closer,

stood on tiptoe and wondered what these tiny
people were doing on top of each other,

stone orgasm chiseled on their faces,
outlasting the dust collecting between their bodies.

Looking closer, I saw their clay sex sweating in
the heat of pyramids, legs and arms twisting

around the god of the sun, a sacrifice of lust,
distorted faces molded from the artist's hands,

one set of figurines dancing a threesome—
two women and one man the sandwich

we have wanted our entire lives, a taste
of dirt from the shelf on my tongue

when I placed my fingers to my lips,
stood back from the Aztecs with

their mud of passion
surviving the great conquest.

BURNING BREAST

for George and Mary Ann

The cancer of history is married to the river
that stole dark sediment from the earth,

the trail to desire moving from body to body,
marking the breast with a kiss from a lover

who bent down to listen.
What he heard smoldered for a lifetime,

until the courage was found to smear mud
from that river onto the burning breast.

When it hurt, the music changed.
When it began to heal, the mud body twisted

in a light not seen since their days began,
a torch hidden in gratitude and weeping,

its wet flame flickering alive.
The cancer is the hourglass of the elements,

each grain made to lift the torso
and set it down again.

When the body rests, the sand blows away.
When the second body washes at the river,

the forest surrounding a charred house
lies down and listens to the moon.

TOUCH

An oil lamp is damaged
by ambition in the spine,

while canyon floors
return me to the burning

city where I saw an old man
lean against a house

in the alley and didn't
know who he was,

his brown hands tracing
patterns on the hard mud.

As I passed him,
he whispered, "Look.

Put your hands here.
This is a beautiful wall."

STONE

George Oppen said the poem
is an object, a decision toward

a concept, like bricks falling
out of a building.

If so, the form of language must
be the blossoming flower rising

inside the man standing
under the broken gates.

When he attended the Altamont Concert
in 1969, Oppen wrote the deafening music

belonged to no one and thousands in
the ravaged crowd were in mourning.

When Oppen crouched in the mud
to listen to the Rolling Stones,

he believed a poem could
survive the electricity because

as he knelt in the bleeding field,
he held a tiny stone in each fist.

THE DONKEY CART APPARITION,
LAS TRUCHAS, NEW MEXICO

It came out of the snow, the black-robed figure
urging the donkey to move faster, the cart
overloaded with skulls and the worn shoes
from dozens of women, a pair of leather ones
falling to the ground as the old beast pulled harder,
its master ignoring me, draped head bowed.

I stood in the dirt street, heard the wooden wheels
roll closer, adobe walls falling down the cliffs to
empty the town, a second person in black limping
across a broken porch, her face lifting from the veil,
resembling my grandmother dead one year.

It was Julia beckoning me to take her from
what I couldn't see, light seeping through
the doors and boarded windows of this shattered
village, winter sun crashing into the pines.
I got into my car, didn't know where to go,

the winding road lighting my way to the mountains,
daring me to follow the cliffs down the chasm of home,
the donkey cart coming after me as I turned to the highway,
looked over my shoulder as the old woman in black
climbed the cart and disappeared in the falling snow.

MEDITATION AT CANUTILLO

Yesterday, in the weeds, I saw a poster
looking for a price and a pistol,
ancestors dying without leaving
a gravestone, though I couldn't
bring them back without driving
to the river to collect twigs, start
a fire and recite from a holy disc
I made when I knew how to rhyme.
The fires are about loss, feet of
the family at the edge of the grave.
The smoke is about home humming
with insects caught on their own,
a meal in the kitchen served before
the will is unfolded and read.

The rain is about tomorrow,
arms of brothers and sisters
dark with what they share in
wanting everyone to go home,
the siren to stop, their loss
turning into a stone calendar
their children can be educated
by during years of poverty,
the rising days of ravens
that won't leave them alone.

There is tripe for the taste
and the burning under.
A fist of mint, sliced onions
hardened with a bitter tongue,
the coyote's hind legs smashed
on the highway to Canutillo,
raising its head in the headlights
before it died.

There was a slaughter in the church
where the priest wore an apron
and never lighted any candles.
By the altar, I heard a whisper that
there is a flag of surrender on
the other side.
Kneeling there, I saw eleven
fingers on my hands—two for
pointing, two for scraping
the bowl, the left hand
for hiding something, all ten
folded into each other because
the eleventh was never there.
Pick one of these—a turbulent
jalapeño in the bowl or a lost dog
safely crossing the street.

Anger in Canutillo turns the streets
from brick to black, flames rioting
for their own sake, buildings surviving
the unrest in a documentary about
a poet evolving into a thinking man,
alphabet dust choking him and trapping
him to change the town.
His brown arms and legs burn with
the suffocating wind as he is slammed
against the door, implosion sending
the house to hell.

Now the scent of tears and cries
basks in mid-afternoon sunlight,
cemeteries awaiting their crosses,
mountains in the distance letting go
of ancestral light, two ceremonies
in progress—one for history,
one for the wind that memorizes
how many mourners appear as

the heavy coffin is carried down
the church steps by old men who
walked across the desert in silence,
their ages revealed in the color of
the flowers surrounding the grave.

LIES

Etruscans used volcanic rock
to personify their deities and
they soon crumbled.
This imperfection changed
history until you stood there,
studying your ashen hands.
By staring at your fingers,
you made sure the guilty
were not forgotten.
Many souls are invisible
but we are too destructive
to believe they are there.

No one has determined why
the legend says it is appropriate
for a beautifully gowned lady
to water a peony or why
a winter plum should be
tended by a silenced monk.
In this mild winter of no snow,
the magnolia in the backyard
is starting to blossom.
If the day freezes, it can die.
If it stays warm, the little girl
in a light sweater can gather
the blossoms and talk to the sun.

Robert Oppenheimer concluded
scientists who set off the first
atomic bomb, 150 miles north
of El Paso, committed eternal sin.
His teacher disagreed,
claiming science does not
determine sin because science

is not a great fire with clouds,
merely a fact.
Oppenheimer was there,
crouching in the fire wind,
goggles aflame.

People lied every day after it was
revealed unknown plants sprouted
from Nazi bomb craters in London
and this was kept secret to not reveal
explosions create the seeds
and the genes of pollens.

Is this worth proving or does lyric
simplicity reign and shadows that
fight the sun win by day's end?
Even the surviving melons in
the garden have something to say
about this, their skins changing color
in the warm air that will not welcome
winter until people quit lying
and start running across the shallow
rivulets of their creative tears.

Can a blind man sense unnatural
faces people paint over their
natural expressions?
If so, there might be fewer liars,
but the boy who crosses the street
is stronger than the boy who hides
behind the tree, waiting for the
army ants to start fighting.
He must know mummified Peruvian
llamas in Paracan graves had five toes
instead of the usual two.

Oppenheimer, did you lie?
The white desert is still there,
the white mountains eroding
without you, their white rocks
resembling the withered wreaths
uncovered every time Egyptian
tombs of gold and diamond-lined
skeletons are excavated, riches
protecting the ancient dead,
hands of an uncovered boy sculpted
in gold, his eyes in obsidian,
the withered wreath the only thing
moving as it senses the warm air
of the opened earth.

CROSSING NEW MEXICO WITH WELDON KEES

after Kees' "Travels in North America"

1. Santa Fe

"The walls are old," he says.
I turn in the plaza and nod to Weldon Kees,
his face as dark as the cool shadows
that surround us, walls keeping him
safe, honoring his silence, though
he comes to me to be led away.

"The mountains out there are not old,"
he claims and slips his hands into his coat.
We cross the street, each Indian blanket
on the ground holding jewelry I would love
to touch, but Kees and the Navajo man
selling his crafts are whispering to the ground.

Kees surprises me by entering the Museum of Arts.
I follow him, the stone floor ringing with
our footsteps, empty arches blending above.
Kees stops and turns to me.
"One can see only so much," he says.

He leads me to the twisted dwarf,
the tangled form of faith and death,
arrows bristling from its muscled body,
a sacrifice of the ugly encased in glass,
Kees staring at the sculpture as if
he knows why we really can't see it.
He points to the deepest arrow
and places a hand on my shoulder.
"When you believe this, you are home,"
he tells me and walks out.

2. Albuquerque

The Sangre de Cristo mountains are old
and he is driving my car to the highest ridge,
the valley below avoiding the bright moon,
the same white light in the bay Kees wanted
to touch before he left.

"Mist and clouds are a lie," he claims.
"Look down there. Men are running away."
He drives slowly to the top and we get out,
the autumn sun burning terraces into scrub
cedars and piñon pines he wrote about
when he crossed here long ago,
standing on the edge of the cliff
as if this is the only way for him to go.

"Look past what you want to see,"
he sighs as the wind takes his slick hair
and makes him into someone
I have seen before, the streets of
Albuquerque down there as dusty
as his closed eyes.

We stand on the edge and I wait
at this elevation with Kees who wrote
that the towns we will not visit are
places where home truly lies.
"I must go," he decides.
"Where to?" I ask.
"Anyplace you haven't seen," he says,
and walks down the mountain.

3. *Tyuonyi*

Kees and I are happy when the sun
splits the tree for a moment because
yesterday controlled this mountain dawn,
burning mud deeper into the adobe.
Cottonwoods catch fire here, give
the people time to hide inside turtle shells,
though they come out to watch us.

I stop as the drawings come to life
under the arches, symbols familiar
to those who sleep by crossing
the street each night.
As I stare, I realize a man who
disappears wants to understand
and not hide, yet the designs
tempt me to walk in the wrong
direction and leave him behind.
To go farther up would mean
a canyon where I have been.

A dirt street inside another path,
tiny houses falling back,
letting me pass beyond their
locked doors, as if the smoking
windows know where I must go.
When I enter the *placita*, the old
woman is not there because this
is about bringing Kees back.
The dirt street opens to the last
scorched tree breaking out of walls
to shade what can't be blessed, its
branches confusing until their cracks
enter the ground in search of peace.

4. Santa Maria

Water disappears to settle as clear glass
that contains memories of thirst,

the ancient hole found in the ruins,
Kees' hand keeping the others from skimming

the surface of the still water, reaching
to be alone under the mountain wall,

though eyes that watch have seen this before,
men entering and never coming out.

One hand keeps the other from touching the surface.
Pulling back allows the echo of falling rocks,

the deep swimmer breaking through walls
to emerge on the other side of the well

where the first figures to emerge in centuries are
sitting and rubbing sand over their wet, shivering bodies.

5. Fort Selden

Kees is getting tired in the desert heat
and sits on a historic slab of western settlement,

this old fort a museum where thirsty men
come to drink from the bitter well.

Kees smokes too many cigarettes
and shakes his head at me,

"Look at the moth and the deep iris in your garden
because the equation I found in San Francisco

is an eclipse drawn on paper
by my trembling hands."

He pauses and takes a drag, my head bathed
in sweat and confusion as he coughs this,

"It is too late because jazz has gone away.
I placed a stone deity of a bird next to an eggplant

on my desk, its smooth purple skin as significant
as the gathering of birds in your head,

their chirping coming from sorrow,
even from the bay where I never told a lie,

though the grand steps lead to the burned church
where the musicians used to trace my forehead."

I stare at him and he tosses smoke on the ground
because we are close to home.

6. El Paso

Kees waits at the bus station
in my hometown.
We cannot go farther because
the border is out there and as violent
as the reasons he disappeared
in San Francisco a long time ago.
I want to tell him who I think he is,
but I grew up here and must hide
how things have really been,
drawing the light off the mountains
as if the doubters of history are simply
starving boys offering to shine Kees'
shoes on the corner of Paisano Street.

My hometown has a bridge,
but Kees won't go near it because
he says to cross it would be
to admit there is something wrong
on the other side of my family's house.
He can never cross because
we have found our way here,
El Paso dreaming its population
of mute men must keep growing
because the border keeps taking
too many of them away.

Kees looks at the bus schedule,
runs out of cigarettes
and everything is closed.
He nods at nothing and waits
on the bench with someone
he swears looks like me.

SNOW FIELDS ON FIRE

*after attending 86-year-old Robert Bly's last public
reading, October 16, 2013, Minneapolis, Minnesota*

The old man walks out of the snow fields
and they are on fire, his father's ashes
smeared across his forehead and cheeks,
his dark face so radiant in the snow.
The white fields of yesterday are frozen so
he can stand there and whisper to the ground.
The old man burns in the flakes, his white hair
bristling with smoke from abandoned cabins
and the last woman he ever loved.

He has another song to tremble to,
but can't remember all the words
when water rushes under the ice beneath
his arms as he falls in, the flames in the fields
dancing to save him, fish him out of the ice
while he still breathes, his arms extended wide,
ice dripping off his hands like the great bear
he always wanted to be.

He is alive in the snow fields that whiten
the heat until his heart is the soul sculpted
out of things he couldn't be—a lantern in
the wind, the coals in the stove, not even
the silent owl hiding in the trees.
He survives the cold plunge and rises from
his bed as he asks, "Who brought me here?"

The snow fields are on fire and he watches
the late moon eat itself in the western night,
his mouth frozen shut because the old man
has settled back in his easy chair, voice quiet,
the fires spreading outside as he closes his eyes

and holds the fire sticks that took the first leaves
into the snowstorm, hands of men that started
this conflagration before leaving him alone.

TO BE

Last night, an old man knew he was
only six or seven years old.
His body told him to take his time,
the car would be arriving soon.

Last night, an old man ate like the pigs
of the world loved him.
His stomach was full, though it hurt,
and made him happy,

his legs circulating the blood of kings.
Last night, an old man loved a woman
and found what he loved brought him happiness,
a way to quit pretending he was done.

Last night, an old man knew he was only
six or seven years old and wrapped
the blankets around himself.

His whispering confession was actually a soul,
and this soul knew how to dance
when the man danced.

Even the village of women whispered
among themselves about his fate as he slept,
gossiping about his belly and the way

he cried out when the unguarded lion
in the plaza got greedy and stood
perfectly still.

THE SACRED FIRE

The soldier returning from the war
is a boy displaced in the leaf-green
water by a shape that appeared without
warning, the breathing of those who
never returned, ammunition belts worn
around the orphaned heart, the orphans
actually his parents staring at an Army
helmet next to a funeral casket.
My nephew Tony told his mother how
he drove his Humvee over an Iraqi child
as an act of survival, then he came home.

The moon rose to be placed in Tony's
mouth during his funeral,
my sister's house filled with his pictures.
He died after his PTSD was out of control,
dozens of medications killing him,
benefits held up, a woman Army general
assuring his mother his country would
help all veterans to get well.
When I couldn't write about this,
howling wind brought snow and
a black cat came to our front door,
neighbors letting it out at night.
Our cat looked through the window
and the two stared at each other
before the black cat left.

My sister says her son is with God
and I want to write about God,
but it is snowing and the white walls
melt in a rare sun, the abstraction of
God helping me gain distance between
history and what I can't understand.

Drawn by a finger in the desert sand,
the route of invasion is as clear as
the day my writing returned.
There are words under the folded flag
and shrapnel will rewrite the books.
A mist hangs outside as I face this,
my ideas avoiding the cemeteries.
The river has never been a part of this.
When I gaze across the peaceful mountains,
I whisper to a child who is going to survive.

CADETS AT THE VIRGINIA MILITARY INSTITUTE READ *HOWL AND OTHER POEMS* BY ALLEN GINSBERG

photo by Gordon Ball

It was the end of the century.
Men with shaved heads.

Men with shaved heads
worshiping the stone.

Men with shiny heads believing
the gun came from the stone.

It was near the end of the calendar.
Teaching them how to listen to the poem,

though the men don their uniforms
to kiss the coldest stone.

Turning the page, a country is
occupied in the new century.

Underlining a passage in question,
the cadets begin to understand.

It was after a long battle.
Naked men with shaved heads

talking among themselves, some not
knowing what happened to the stone.

THE WAR MUSEUM

Now that the war is over, I can build my war museum,
place my dead nephew's uniform there,

along with white hairs from Saddam's last beard,
a crumb from the corn chip George Bush choked on,

a McDonald's burger wrapper from the biggest
PX on a military base in the world,

mount a news headline or two from U.S. papers
that wanted to tell the whole truth,

though I haven't been able to find one and settle,
instead, for a video from FOX news.

In the war museum,
I would turn off the switch to Dick Cheney's

pacemaker and hook it up to a coin machine
for tourists to try and keep him alive,

my own version of this weapon of mass
destruction funding me so I can search

for rare asphalt from an American street
where a protester might have marched,

build a display of names, not of battlefield
casualties, but thousands of Army suicides,

nightmares never counted on websites
wanting to list the whole truth.

In the war museum, I would release photos of
my family, before and after, blame their evolution

on American history, display closeups of their faces
as maps of where our country has gone, include

a photo of my nephew's last girlfriend, the one
who found him lifeless in his apartment and,

unfortunately, looks like the woman in uniform
bowing over the naked Iraqi in the lights of Abu Ghraib.

THE DESTROYER OF COMPASSES

The destroyer of compasses is my brother.
He lies in the wet fields of war and dies young,
rises above the soil to be trapped in the great
books that tell the story because magnetic north
has been demolished, the master of compasses
witnessing the coffin and flag draped with
weeping mothers and the lying generals that
perform without the compass
turning their sweat to blood.

The destroyer of compasses is my brother.
He eats the same meal as I, though
the bird of migration is trapped in its cage
and cannot flee, its cry waking the young
and resolving the old. When the bird is eaten,
the boy takes its compass apart, hiding
the magnetic bone in his left ear,
leaving the blazing feathers behind.

The destroyer of compasses wants to be
my brother, but I am too old for advice,
the glass on the compass touched by
our fathers who doubted its magic—
devices hidden in the shoes of the men
who drink to their angry sons, loyal
followers, and the boys who defend
the country at any price.

The destroyer of compasses is my brother.
He lifts the sorrow of lies beyond the fields
of rock where the compass refuses to work,
the instrument spinning wildly before
the young man is told where he is bound,
orders given in secret because the circle

of young men will not stop spinning
until it finds the magnetic point.

MY NEPHEW'S ARMY HELMET

The lone image
I keep seeing from

the funeral is his
camouflaged Army helmet

sitting on a pedestal
alongside his open casket.

I can't get it
out of my head—

an Army helmet as
a deep bowl of sorrow

unable to protect the soul
that has lifted through

the clouds to a ceasefire
with heaven.

Part Three

THREE UNFINISHED MASTERPIECES

Marcel Duchamp

The brain is embedded in stone and the chain resembles a baby being born, but his hands have sculpted before, so the incomplete birth brings a cloud onto the worktable and several hammers fall to the floor, the form of guessing hardened into an entrance toward oblivion where the outstretched shoulder blades are actually a man running away from his bird because his lover did not chisel the stone, but collected the shards instead.

Max Ernst

It can only be described by its title—"The Susceptible Virgin Opening Her Dress to White Whales While the Investigation of the Balloon Brings Madness to the Forefront of the Ear Where the Priest Embeds Arrows into His Waiting Savior." This forgotten work Ernst abandoned when the war came used to be called "Eight Rubber Bands Stretched in the Queen's Butter Before Her Black Stocking Was Removed by the Winter Wind." After Ernst changed the title, he fled.

Paul Klee

The orange flowers on the wall allow the piercing study of a hand puppet Klee did not finish because he couldn't find the puppet's head. It resided in his studio, but the cloth head disappeared one night after the last thunderstorm that enveloped Klee's village. He had spent six days making the tiny head out of pieces of cloth, string, and unknown objects. When the head disappeared and the remaining sheath of the body fit on Klee's right hand, it did not look like a headless puppet. When Klee held his hand up in the air, it resembled a glove Klee used to wipe the tears off the face of the one he loved.

MAX ERNST WITH HIS COLLECTION OF KACHINAS. NEW YORK. 1936

The painter stole some of them but history
has forgiven him because Max Ernst burns

in a mixed haze of color, disfigurement, and
the deepest claws of the demon that eats him.

His Kachina dolls surround him, white-haired
artist in white furs kneeling among gods who

never look at him, their masked eyes peering
down the tunnel where Ernst is tortured by

several naked women he painted years before.
The Kachinas stand still as the canyon walls

reach out to Ernst and touch him, the corn
doll removing his hunger, Patung the squash

kachina suddenly stuffing him with squash
until Ernst throws everything up, the dolls

covered in his internal agony, the photographer
never capturing this because he fled the room

when Ernst could not stop heaving, the floor
and walls covered in new life, the splattered

blossoms making him lie down in the canyon
until his collection of dolls dry in the sun

and become the twisted rocks Ernst has to
keep painting, over and over again.

RENÉ CHAR PAINTS ON A PIECE OF BARK DURING A NIGHT OF INSOMNIA

René Char paints on a piece of bark on a night of not being able to sleep. His two new poems are written on paper tucked in his jacket, though he paints on bark to keep the others from seeing what he will hide near the railroad tracks. Perhaps he will remember to retrieve it after the war is over, but he knows things will never end and the charcoal will fade in the rain. René Char paints on bark as he waits inside the tiny room, the candlelight flickering across his hands. He cannot sleep for the third night in a row and the drawing is what he has seen in the dark hours when the words have stopped and the distant sound of gunfire has brought a pattern he traces on the rough bark. René Char blows the candle out, feels the pistol in his jacket, and paints blind. His fingers follow the road from the farmhouse where he was born to the intricate face of his mother. He paints in blackness because it is the path to preserving the true design of what he has seen in years of resistance, his poems the only things he will carry with him when he joins the others across the river.

THE SOUL CAN'T PAINT ITSELF

William Carlos Williams' 1950s poem
about El Paso, two alligators in
the plaza fountain when I was a kid.

Two alligators staring at him as
he crosses the international bridge
to touch things on the other side.

Naked Juarez whore dancers discovering
the desert place and pulling the poet inside
so he can write about the donkey show.

Decades before the violence, hawks sing.
Childhood when the earth thought it was
sober but the doctor examined otherwise.

WC Williams seeing hundreds of sparrows
in city park trees shitting on running men,
hometown bird shit I can't remember.

BALD EAGLE NORTH OF SHELBY, MONTANA

We spot it from a hundred yards away,
our car throwing dust across the dirt road,
the huge eagle perched atop a telephone pole,
empty prairie and distant mountains bringing
us closer, the bald eagle waiting for us.

The bird grows larger as sunlight
flashes across the wires, a message
reaching us in the middle of nowhere,
the closest town eighty miles away,
yellow fields empty of trees and
the eagle must have a place to go
when it lifts and spreads.

Years ago, I found a dead hawk
on my trek through Cochito Canyon,
came upon it sweaty and out of breath,
the valley below opening like a green
blanket, the brown and white feathers
of the hawk bristling with ants that
carried its secret into the earth.

When we returned home from
Montana, I couldn't see it clearly.
When I thought about what it was,
the empty road stayed that way.
When I looked again, getting near
the eagle was only a moment
on a dirt road.

It was the hiker staying in the canyon
to practice the story of the eagle and
the hawk, so he could descend.
That day near Shelby, I slowed the car
and dust covered us in a cloud.
The eagle sprang off the wires,
its wings shadowing the car,
rising beyond our sight, pebbles on
the gravel road ringing against
our vehicle as we moved.

I left the dead hawk in the canyon
those many years past,
haven't told anyone its tiny head
was gone, the mutilated hawk visiting
me in a dream where I paused
and turned into the trees, calling
myself names someone called
me long ago, those wings
ascending in a different light
because the road to the eagle
had always been there.

THE PLAIN OF HOOVES

Imagine horses thundering over the horizon,
Spanish invaders riding them through the people
while a deity withstands the blind centuries,
the drawing "The Plain of Hooves" by Emilio Zorra
Morales melting its dogs and dancing children into
blessed creatures that alight on his father when
he smells of the first whore, the fourth one pouring
hot oil on his back, his tattoo of a blue panther
changing into Morales' caved bats and blue insects.

The canvas withers in the heat because Morales
was consumed by those howling dogs, the plains
littered with battle horses, the face of Morales' father
emblazoned on a wall where his face was scratched
with the first rock his son held, the artist leaving
his mother with one foot in the valley, his father's
enormous penis in the painting avoiding the angel
on horseback, plucking the eyebrows of God.

THE DRUMS

I banged on an Indian drum
to fight my depression, found
it on my assigned chair,
hospital therapy including this
healing session, percussion
instruments everywhere, a dozen
sick people grabbing tambourines
or sitting with bongos, one wild-haired
young man choosing an upright
bass drum, the patients ready to
beat their deep and scary
sadness with their hands.
I set my drum between weak
knees and felt self-conscious
as the therapist told us when to
come in, what rhythm to keep.
We started playing and the power
of the drums went up my open
palms and into my jumping heart.
I closed my eyes and the group
pounded harder, everyone forgetting
the instructions, hitting our own
beat, whatever we called up
arriving nearby, sweat pouring
down our faces as we pounded
faster and faster, the sound one
rhythm in the shaking room
because the depressed drummers
knocked down the locked door
and a great presence gave in to
our thunder and entered.

HOSPITAL

I paced the hallway of the locked mental ward for days,
counted the laps as the pills made me turn and turn,
other patients passing by in their darkness, my black
hole getting deeper with no exit, my cold room and
white bed like icebergs floating past before the sea
crashed against the rocks and a man I used to know
vanished in the mist.

Group therapy in a room full of women meth heads,
suicidal young men, older male alcoholics, and me,
the long table of people nodding off or rocking,
afraid to look up, my thoughts disappearing quickly,
waiting for my turn to admit I worked too hard for
years, burned out and kept in here, my words
puzzling the others because they said it sounded like
there was absolutely nothing wrong with me.

The nurses sedated me with two pills and I slept
like I wasn't there, woke groggy and unknown,
staggered to the nurse's station to get a cup of coffee,
the ward still sleeping because others were more sedated
on four or five pills at bedtime, others pacing hallways
as if the night would never come and go.

They medicated me so I could stop falling, quit annihilating
myself with the quiet force of a mute weapon that had
no shape as it turned my thoughts into lethal riddles that
whispered, "Go away." When I slept, I did not remember
dreams, though I saw an old woman watering a garden
with a green hose and never looked up, flowers turning
into the sudden beam of a flashlight, the nurse checking
on me once an hour to see if I was still there.

I doodled and drew pictures, sat at a table by myself,
created images out of my head, depression attracting
a circus of twisted faces that played for hours, undecipherable
mazes and mandalas that cured me as they filled my pad,
drawing maps with borders around no man's land,
puzzles that helped me with their beautiful shapes.

My white book was stolen from the white room
in the white corridor where I wore a white robe.
My dreams were turning white like the blank pages
of the book I set on the table next to my bed.
When I awoke in the morning, I couldn't find it.
I tried to write in its pages the night before,
but couldn't spell or read one sentence inside
the paperbacks my wife brought me.

I wanted to write my name, but couldn't focus
when I clutched the pen in my fingers and
scratched on a sheet, the mark blessing the book
that showed up the next day. I heard its sheets
rustle in the dark, opened my eyes to see a form
of survival returning my ability to read and write.

After one week, they said I could leave,
the shrink at his desk proclaiming I was doing
better as he sipped his giant McDonald's Coke
through a straw, my wife and granddaughter
waiting outside, and I didn't know if it was
night or day, though the sun lit up their hearts
as the nurse unlocked the door and I emerged.

NICANOR PARRA

Someday, the great white hair
of the poets will be a sign
the streets have turned.
The 102-year-old poet will stop
in the middle of the path,
hold up his left hand, and cry,
"The confluence of the hands
is divine, but get your long
hair out of your eyes."
Parra will not ask you to cut
it because his poems foretell
of a prophet in search of poets
with long white hair, those
ropes from heaven cut on
the day he wrote his first poem,
the penance for writing being
an eternal sentence of white letters,
syllables and clouds older than
the one who stands in the middle
of the road, directing heaven to
consider its invisible alphabet.

VIOLINS

I quit humming my favorite rock-and-roll songs.
Lately, I hum violin tunes, classical runs and rhythms,
my wife's violin lessons resonating in my head,
two years of learning to play bringing a different
music into my head, my discovery of the violin
making me unplug amplifiers because I love
the open heaven of my wife's violin.

I catch myself humming tunes I don't know,
a Russian master, David Oistrakh, performing on
a black-and-white film from 1937, his Tchaikovsky
Concerto for Violin and Orchestra in D major
the first composition I pay attention to, the DVD
of historic Moscow performances making me
straighten my rock CD collection downstairs
where our two cats hide each time my wife plays.

I am happily interrupted by my six-year-old
granddaughter and her tiny violin, what she has
learned the past year reminding me, at that age,
all I knew was air guitar and glowing dials
on late night radio. Now, I keep humming
"Twinkle Little Star," the song my granddaughter
practices for months, the notes sending me
to her recital where she performs in the flowers
that blossom with each lesson she takes.

I have quit singing rock songs when I am alone.
They are sacred, private data on my iPod.
I listen to my wife practice her violin upstairs
and believe instruments of family are movements
for the heart, my guitars and drums waiting for
the curtain to go up again, the violins of age
and discovery composing a sonata for what
we hear on instinct and what we need to learn.

17-YEAR-OLD ROBERT ZIMMERMAN ATTENDS A BUDDY HOLLY CONCERT IN DULUTH, MINNESOTA, JANUARY 31, 1959

In three days, Buddy Holly will die in a plane crash in
a frozen Iowa cornfield, but tonight Bobby Zimmerman
is in the first-row crowd, watching his hero sing
"Peggy Sue," "That'll Be the Day," and other songs
Bobby tries to pound on the old piano in the Hibbing
High auditorium, sneaking in when he can.
Later, Bobby will swear to his friends that Buddy Holly
looked right at him and waved at the end of "Peggy Sue."
Buddy Holly shouts, "Goodnight, Duluth!" as the lights
come on, the kid jumping up and down as cheers
resound from northern Minnesota to Iowa.

Imagine Bob Dylan at one of Buddy Holly's last
concerts, the clichés about the torch being passed,
though the kid doesn't really know what took place—
music and oncoming death, songs starting in Duluth
that night when Bobby stepped into the freezing air,
two friends he brought not saying much because
they are thinking about Holly, an icy drive back home.

"Buddy was great!" Bobby keeps repeating.
"Yeah," one mutters. "Open the door! I'm freezing!"
the other yells and yanks on the locked car door,
the crowd passing by. Imagine Bob Dylan driving
his parent's car from Hibbing to Duluth to see
Buddy Holly, then the journey home, the kid
taking his time unlocking the doors, gazing at
the crowd, cold hands in his pockets because
his fingers are on fire.

BOB DYLAN'S NEWPORT GUITAR

1

Where is Bob Dylan's electric guitar?
Is it still plugged in at Newport, 1965?
Did rock and roll change because the young
man in dark glasses wept backstage after
the folk crowd booed and taunted him?
Why ask these questions now when Dylan
is an old man, the cord to his guitar
traded for the key to heaven long ago?
The woman who claims she has
the guitar says her father, the pilot,
found it in back of Dylan's plane.
Dylan's people insist he has it and
it never left his side after the show.

2

I have Dylan's guitar from Newport.
It comes out of my speakers every day.
I listen to his acoustic songs, then
switch to electric tunes to realign
what came before, Michael Bloomfield
laying down vicious runs as Dylan wails,
"I ain't gonna work on Maggie's Farm no more."
I own the instrument he used back then,
hiding it in my speakers for forty-seven years,
the '64 Stratocaster wrapped in dreams
we had before Dylan turned up the volume
and the country went insane.

3

Dylan's guitar is right here, instrument
of personal secrets and fame.
The sunburst design might be an image
of Dylan's brain, his notorious way of
staying ahead of the game to trick fans
who worship him, along with those
who tried to cut the power cord
with axes to silence the crowd.
Even the small amplifier Dylan used
buzzed in low defiance because it
was dismantled for spare parts when
Dylan went to England with The Band.

The guitar from Newport now
hangs on my wall because the last
Dylan album I bought has a song
with a secret line no one gets to
decipher in my name.
When he plays it for me,
I possess what no rock star
can express or take away.
I have kept the guitar for most
of my life and it has been safe.
Years ago, when I discovered
why he went electric, I polished
the instrument with fine oil and
kept staring at it that day.

4

Are you searching for Dylan's
guitar he plugged into Newport
as the beginning of the end?
How can I call it that when Dylan

composed eternal songs the guitar
electrified to shock him on stage?
Dylan's tears short-circuited the pickups,
his acoustic second half at Newport
not the legend it could have been
because he came back out under
the lights, a shiny face honoring
the tradition, smoking fingers
sparking with a rage that almost
scorched his acoustic guitar.

DUANE ALLMAN WITH THE CROSS

In the photo taken a few weeks
before he died, Duane wears

a necklace with a cross on his neck,
the sweat pouring down his chest

as his guitar streaks the air with smoke,
the concert crowd moving closer as

the long song extends beyond what
the band plays, the look on Duane's

closed eyes and soaked face forgotten
for a moment as his slide guitar propels

"Mountain Jam" beyond breathless
moments because the cross hanging

on Duane's neck is the sacrifice
for bringing the song to its end.

CAPTAIN BEEFHEART LEAVES HIS BODY

Don Van Vliet, January 15, 1941–December 17, 2010

Captain Beefheart leaves his body
and the crow with one eye blows his harp
while Big Joan sets up, though her hands
are too small to touch the moon that spreads
itself over Don Van Vliet's closed eyes.
Captain Beefheart leaves his body
as his China pig steps lightly over the feathers
of the parakeet that smokes a strange pipe
and sings to the Captain to wake up.
Van Vliet smiles in his brickyard sleep,
waves to the dagger in the record
executive's heart, though he is not guilty
because he buttered his toast on
the last day of his wheelchair.

Captain Beefheart leaves his body
and Zoot Horn Rollo blisters his fingers
on the burning guitar he found in
Beefheart's clay casket, the tiny lawn
mowers in Rollo's breath inviting
the audience of scarecrows and Don's
worn socks to enter the chapel.
When his body is kissed goodbye,
Captain Beefheart opens his eyes
and catches two flower petals
he inserts in each nostril, growls
that heaven will smell better
when he blows the crow's harp
on the other side.

INVISIBLE GUITAR

for George Kalamaras

The invisible guitar is strummed
on the memory train of old

turntables and dusty vinyl,
the torn speaker fitting the jams

where the guitar solo is played
by the first guitarist to discover

the missing finger of Jerry Garcia
was actually a guitar pick stolen by God.

DRIVING AROUND EL PASO, MARVIN GAYE'S "WHAT'S GOING ON" COMES ON THE RADIO

Ashes from the Gila Wilderness fire descend on
El Paso, coat my car in white as Marvin Gaye sings,

"Brother, brother, brother, we don't need to escalate."
I turn on the windshield wipers and drive past

the old Coliseum where I saw him in concert,
the building standing half a century later.

I don't know which street to turn on as Marvin
says there are too many mothers crying.

I want to go to the cemetery where my nephew lies,
the song reminding me of Iraq and how he died.

I drive around El Paso as Marvin asks,
"What's going on? What's going on?"

I weep for a hometown I don't recognize,
dust from New Mexico cleansing the town,

leading me to the street where my father went
down, emerging on the other side to forgive him

as pure ashes wash his outstretched hands.
Marvin Gaye comes on the radio because

familiar buildings are gone, crumbling streets
leading to graffiti walls where a timeless song

is an oath to what went wrong, how the town
stays the same, Marvin's voice of a city angel

who answers questions by driving with me
and never showing me a wrong turn.

ZODIACAL LIGHT

The faint glow that passes through the constellations
of the zodiac in the morning and evening skies,
a book as old as fire and water, the yellow pages
between the hands, the book dropped in the middle
of the street, its brittle pages forming a new text.
Cicadas invaded, then it finally rained.
Dust particles sweeping off comets create the light,
contribute to the brightness of a corona, a blinking
eye reading how a Mixtec sacrificial ceremony
brought an enormous shadow over the bloody
pyramid because any footprint would do.
It wasn't until 1916 that a lesson on memory
was introduced to the room full of empty chairs,
a diary entry on the zodiac printed on handmade
paper, the letters formed on large blocks of wood,
the limited edition of the calendar stored in a warehouse
for ninety-two years until a green lake was conceptualized
and a shift in starlight was revealed by observations
of a solar eclipse, the rhythms of the railroad train
and a purple sheet of paper where a woman bled
an abstract pattern for her lover, her scratched eye
watering and accidentally filling with one loose
eyelash, pages of origami for the left foot and
the telescope observing how light interacts with
gravity so the kneeling man loses his identity papers
and is prevented from fleeing the country.
Two sweating and dripping large breasts, people
raising their children without religion because zodiacs
are too troublesome and force evacuation after
a rain of toads turns into a storm of handkerchiefs,
each falling hankie a meditation on the creaking
of human bones, the smell of yellow stains on
the dying manuscript, capture of dignity involving
star dust appearing on photostatic copies in 1923,

the coffee cup and locked trunk surviving the fire,
the habitation of old wounds charted by the lone
man tracing an engraving of a constellation onto
an ancient sheet of copper.

THE FACE OF THE SUN

for Larry Levis

The face of the sun is a myth.
We are the ones who sing
over our parents' sleeping bodies.
When Emiliano Zapata's two white
horses escaped from the corral,
it was a sign he would be killed that day.

When the white face of the sun
is revealed, it changes the myth
into a story where our parents,
in their bedroom, never wake up.
At last, our childhood home, we think.
Our empty house, at last.

Your eyes wake in the morning
of the white light and you leave,
though you are the one who wants
to stay, but you know the white horse
that stays is riderless.

HAIR

*César Vallejo never died, the canyon was as full of him as
the Tao is full of butterflies.*
—Gonzalo Rojas

Twenty years ago, I sat on a park bench
on a warm spring day.
Suddenly, a plain-looking butterfly
alighted on my right shoulder.
Startled, I turned my head
and the butterfly flew away.
It touched me for five seconds,
its dull, brown wings showing me
a parchment never written on.

Nothing has landed on
my shoulders since, though
César Vallejo whispered to me once,
"Carry it home and I can empty your hands of guilt."

A few days after the butterfly,
he sat next to me and took off his hat
before telling me his hair was falling out,
though his wife had been collecting strands of it
for years to make a pillow for their bed.

Pablo Neruda asked these questions before he died:

Where did the sea come from?
How many times have I drowned?
Who saved me seven times?
Did the bells ring to announce
I was done with the earth?
Why can't birds ever be turned around?

Did the first woman take her first step
toward the first man or toward the blinding sun?
Why do animals hide in places I have never been?
How many rain clouds does it take
for the language of grief to disappear?

Why do my hands tremble in sunlight
and lie peacefully folded in the dark?
How often does sand blown in the wind
drift to the other side of the world?
Who was the first man to get a grain
of dust caught in his eye?

Where did the first teardrop fall?
When does the silent crow land
in the tree and when does it flee?
When does the silent owl alight
into the moon and when does it return?
Who named me Pablo and why should
I believe it was her?

Why does the dirt road pretend the earth is flat?
When did the first library burn?
What was the last book to go up in flames?
How many musical instruments does a seashell contain?
Where do I go when the trail of a falling white star
resembles strands from my mother's hair?

MAX JACOB'S LEATHER COAT
AND THE POSSIBILITY OF GRIEF

On the day the Gestapo came and took him away, the last three prose poems he was writing were left at the kitchen table along with his old leather coat that hung on the chair, until Jacob's landlord entered the room and grabbed it. One can retrace the history of the coat and notice the silhouette of a man sitting at the kitchen table without the coat that accompanied him all over Paris. The last three poems he wrote in freedom were about the leather coat because the sheets were found two weeks later by the young woman who rented Jacob's apartment. When she entered the kitchen for the first time, she picked up the pieces of paper, but did not know how to read, so she set the poems on the dirty table and went to inspect the other room. Max Jacob's last three poems before he was taken away by the Nazis were finally read by the figure sitting at the table, alone and bent over, squinting at the tiny handwriting, his leather coat worn tightly on his shoulders.

JACK KEROUAC BRINGS HIS MOTHER TO THE MEXICAN BORDER, 1957

1

After a twenty-four-hour bus ride from New Orleans,
Jack Kerouac and his mother Gabrielle
must wait four hours in El Paso and he decides
to show her Juarez across the river,
the last stop before they get to California.
Jack wants his mother to enjoy herself,
unaware it is the last time he will share
an adventure with her.
They walk one mile to the "little bridge"
as Jack calls it and a few blocks into Juarez
where the road spirit returns.
They pay three cents each to cross into Mexico.

2

The Franklin Mountains sleep behind them,
the Rio Grande and El Paso unaware Jack
and his mother are in the border town that
doesn't believe in heroes or the way lost
writers pass through, whoring and drinking
and staring drunk into the river.

They want Mexican visions the worm
in the mescal bottle never gives because
some fall in the water before the rattlesnake
strikes and gives magic to their voices.
Jack brings Gabrielle into the desert wind,
an act the Beats would dig—the wild rider
showing his mother the flame he found
in the desert the last time he came through,

admitting later in his writings how funny
it was to show his mother another world.

3

They enter the church of La Virgen de
Guadalupe, the Juarez smell of beer,
lime peels, horse and dog shit left behind
as Jack and his mother stare at a *penitente*,
the old man kneeling on the concrete floor
with his arms outstretched, Jack telling her
the wrinkled figure does not want to be
forgiven by a god that doesn't speak.

"Light a candle for Papa," Jack's mother says.
Her son hesitates when he sees one of
the saint statues move its head and stare
down at him, the savior pointing to Jack's
mother, the stirring in the church throwing
Jack to the day he woke outside the church
of El Sagrado Corazón in south El Paso,
the barefoot Mexican boy staring down
at him, Jack hungover on the sidewalk,
the boy's nose running snot, his lovable
face making Jack sit up and reach out
to him, a police car slowly going by,
the boy running into the church.

4

The last time Jack wandered the streets
of El Paso and Juarez, the bowl of *menudo*
he ate one morning made him see,
tripe as hallucinogen as outrageous
as the man that gave Jack a gift in the alley

behind Lucha's Cantina—a shimmering eye
the headless man claimed Jack needed,
a voice warning him each time Jack blinks
shall be one less wish the desert rewards him.

5

Jack blinks and opens his eyes to his mother
nodding at a thin Indian woman on her
knees, moving slowly on the concrete
floor toward the altar, carrying a baby
in her arms as she struggles to keep her
balance, Jack's mother whispering
to her, then abruptly standing back.

"What are you doing?" Jack asks, his voice
echoing through the dark walls of fear,
the empty church shimmering in the heat,
the Indian advancing toward the cross.
His mother turns to Jack.
"What has happened there?" she cries,
her voice booming in the dusty air.
"That poor lil mother has done no wrong.
Is her husband in prison?
She's carrying that leetle baby!"

6

Jack stares at the two moons above the desert,
his left foot no longer bleeding, the sweat on
his face as cold as the burned roses he saw
boiling on the adobe walls, the naked whore
asleep inside, his journal thrown under
the bed, spilled Tequila making him drop
it there, the woman waking the next day

without knowing she slept above lost
writing by Jack Kerouac, poems for the moon
he thought fell into the river when he peered in.

7

Mother and son light candles at the altar
and put dimes in the church box, the wind
filling the church with dust through the open
doors, the sunlight crossing the pews, its
burning beam searching row by row.
Jack's mother will never forget the woman
with her baby and the way she progressed
on her knees, Jack claiming she prayed for
the Indian for many years.

8

The mother figure comes closer.
He opens his eyes without blinking,
the dust of angels on his face, her trembling
fingers making signs he doesn't know,
the blue mountains farther away than
he ever dreamed, each lizard on the wall
taking him to a notebook he found on
the floor, a woman in robes weeping
for him, the melting asphalt of the road
to Las Cruces steaming with lines and
fragments on torn pages he leaves behind.

9

Mother and son wander the plaza,
buy ice cream and sit in the park facing

the El Paso skyline across the river.
Gabriella tries to talk to an Indian couple
on a bench next to them, but they act afraid.
She gives them cigarettes and repeats after them,
"*Chihuahua. Vengo de Chihuahua.*"
Jack spots an old man with caged birds
and recalls enough Spanish to understand
if you pay one peso, you can choose
a bird that will give you your fortune.
"What?" his mother shrugs off the bird man.
"Let's try it," Jack insists. "Give him a peso."
His mother doesn't know what that is,
so Jack takes a coin out of his pocket
and points to a canary in its cage.
The bird doesn't peck at the slip of paper
because the old man hands it to Jack.
Garbriella opens it and reads aloud,
"You will have good *fortuna* with one
who is your son who love you. Say the bird."
Gabriella looks at her son, "How does that
canary know this?"

10

She shakes her head as the sun rises higher
and the smells of the border return.
One more hour and their bus will leave.
Jack and his mother start the walk back
across the bridge, the *Federales* smiling at
her and staring at Jack as they cross.

Jack saw his mother tuck the slip into her
purse and wonders what she will do with it,
mother and son waiting in the El Paso bus
station, the desert breaking in the hot wind,
the highway west to Los Angeles built for

the bus that hits the afternoon fire in the sky
as mother and son cross the desert, forgetting
the smells of tomorrow, songs of lost birds
in the arroyos making Jack open his window
to listen to something besides the low
rhythm of his mother's snores.

SATELLITE

I wanted to spot a satellite among the stars,
but the constellations burned instead,
my place high on the mountain chosen by
the night sky that was black and sparkling,
each point of light marking old guilt,
seconds of vertigo brought on by pulling
my head straight back, The Milky Way
changing course as I fell and stood there,
the northern Colorado forest sinking
below the galaxy that gave me time to be
grateful, pretend I knew how to grasp at
stars I had not seen in years of city living.

I wanted to see a satellite in the midst of
hearing the silent hammer, a distraction
from believing I had a philosophy to cast
light on what blessed me from above.
All I saw was the night that held
something I wanted to believe in,
holding it high above so I could be lost
then located on the porch of a house
on a mountain in a huge, western place
that kept bleeding stars as if there was
no wound deep enough for being alive.

TWO HAWK SKIES IN MINNESOTA

1

A hawk flies over my house in the rain,
landing on the huge alder in the back
where it took a squirrel weeks ago,
its wings vanishing in the rain as if
they were never there, the black line
of flight escaping from my thoughts.
It brought back Robinson Jeffers'
"Hurt Hawks" where he tried to mend
the broken wing of a bird that hated him
in silence, Jeffers releasing it
by the sea to heal itself.

A hawk flew over my house
and I wanted to find movement in
the trees, but their dripping leaves
left a bright entrance where low
clouds drifted as something else,
the hawk in the rain as mute as
Jeffers admitting it was men he hated,
the war years wrinkling his face,
the agony of pushing rocks that built
his house the way I collect wet leaves
in my hands when I am met
by a cold mist that has something
to do with my freedom and
the bird that bristles overhead.

2

It is better to be wrong and watch the hawk
cross the snowfield in a black second,

its wings sharp as the eye that
waits for tomorrow's words.

It is nothing new, how it flies farther away
until I can't see where I am going,

the highway blinded by snow, filaments of passion
pointing away from the nearest fog,

the moment the fox darts across the road
and I close my eyes and make a wish.

It is better to pay attention to the chevron
flight of geese forgotten when the pines

fall into themselves, a grove of them mistaken
for a place to hide, the hawk reappearing overhead

when I get out of the car, shiver in the wind
as I wait for the arrival of what will save me.

THE EDGE OF THE WILDERNESS,
NORTHERN COLORADO

What steps do I take to leave the dirt road?
Invisible footprints must save me.
No one needs to know because no one waits
on the other side of the trees, though
the rumor of mountain lions makes me
wonder what happened to the first man
who entered and saw what was there—
twisted timbers and a farther way in,
the music of chance and breaking twigs,
hidden birds with warnings that
say there is someone behind me.
There is no one to send me in
the right direction, pines growing
thicker as I hesitate and listen
to my hands because my fingers
look at and feel the trees
that creak in the wind.

When a child was lost for days,
his hands were sore from grabbing sticks
and collecting stones, the sound of cars
distant and searching, until the trail
opened and he was home.
I step in the mud and watch for snakes,
though the rocks click alone,
the earth beneath slowly sinking
as I pass and meet black soil
at the drop-off, the river way below
signaling I must turn back,
though the cliff edge of the past brings
hope, the trek into the heart that wears
no feathers, a pounding in my ears

echoing off the aspens whose white
trunks turn me away and I find
a deer bone on the ground.

THE DANCE

The dance where old fathers can't move,
choking on their feet with rhythms of sin
and abandonment, this waltzing of the guilty
sparkling on the streets and inside purple
houses they love to enter.
The men shuffle as if their world will
never end, the sound of their shoes
sliding on concrete as slippery as they
will ever get.

The dance where fathers lie and abandon
their families for women on the other side,
the perfume and high heels overpowering
them to move on cheap beds where rhythm
of the springs enters their heads to make
them wish they had left home long ago.

The dance of the young son waiting
for his father to come home from work,
trading places at the front window with
his mother each hour until, at midnight,
she swears the old man was working
late selling cars for bread on the table—
this cliché as old as the car that finally
pulls up in the darkness as the next
dance is about to begin.

I ONCE KNEW THE BLACK RIDER

after César Vallejo

I once knew the black rider,
but he quit coming to me after

I ate a rare meal with my father,
the old hunchback anorexic-thin

and wrinkled, crunching his lettuce
in silence as he avoided my eyes.

The black rider rode his black horse
in circles, fear boiling inside me

the way my father's body
smoked on his deathbed,

turning to ashes before my eyes as
I reached down to touch his heart.

Now, my blackened fingers trace lines
on my face that never wash away

and my head sweats each time I hear
a galloping sound that never arrives.

HUNCHBACK

My 83-year-old father
I had not seen in eight years

is now a hunchback,
his spine bent forward,

the tall man I used to know
now leaning toward

the ground as if asking
for forgiveness.

A PERIOD OF ASHES

You live in a period of ashes
and they fall day and night,
delicate layers disappearing
as they hit the ground,
the black earth underneath
building in secret.

You love in a period of ashes,
though the naked bodies are being
rained on as they come, black lines
painting lust on bare shoulder blades,
leaving them in exhausted sleep.

You are lost in a period of ashes,
your hair black at birth, though
your way through the trees
is marked by a light that says
if you open your mouth
and hold out your tongue,
the taste of ash will forgive you.

You emerge from the ashes,
lucky they did not fall in your eyes,
years of seeing darkened by something
that used to be there and left when
you blinked with a blackened face,
no longer surprised.

THE THEORY AND PRACTICE OF LOVE

If we could have that face,
we would never grow up.

If we could understand,
we would hide in the trees

and wait for a voice
to bring us back.

If we could recall what
we once had, we would

rhyme the word shape
with the word twig.

We would pretend
a wave of uncertainty

was merely love asking
for room to breathe.

If we could trace a face, we would
reconsider the neck and chest,

wondering where the train was bound
with the old couple sleeping inside.

THE RICHES

The riches of the city echo
like treason minus desire,

dimensions of grass inside the leaf,
beauty inflicted and pained because

the desert is sick of being written about,
imagination fed on bones of angels,

those limbs now petrified because what
is left in the old house where I was born

is the shiniest nail hammered
into the wooden floor.

ACKNOWLEDGMENTS

The author thanks the editors of the following publications where these poems appeared:

American Poetry Review: "Crossing New Mexico with Weldon Kees";

Barrow Street: "One El Paso, Two El Paso";

Bitter Oleander: "Paul Celan's Ashes," "Max Jacob's Leather Coat and the Possibility of Grief," "René Char Paints on a Piece of Bark During a Night of Insomnia," parts of "The Mud Angels, Mesilla, New Mexico" and "To Be";

Caliban: "Bald Eagle North of Shelby, Montana," "Captain Beefheart Leaves His Body," "Give History a Chance," "I Once Knew the Black Rider," "Las Brujas de La Union, New Mexico," "Last Night," "The Face of the Sun," "Snow Fields on Fire," and "They Call the Mountain Carlos";

Carnegie Mellow Review: "Sticky Monkey Flowers, Monterey Bay";

Drunken Boat: "Church";

Fifth Wednesday Journal: "Antlers in the Tree, Livermore, Colorado" and "Stone";

Great River Review: "The Border Is a Line" and "The Sacred Fire";

Interrupture: "The Lynching Postcard, Duluth, Minnesota";

Jet Fuel Review: "A Period of Ashes";

Laurel Review: "Driving Past a Missile Silo Near Langsden, North Dakota";

Malpais Review: "A Judge Orders the Opening of Federico García Lorca's Grave," "Hummingbird on the Porch," "Gods in the Attic," "Landscape Is an Abstraction," and "Again";

Mi POesias: "The Plain of Hooves";

New American Writing: "Cadets at the Virginia Military Institute Read *Howl and Other Poems* by Allen Ginsberg";

Red Rock Review: "The Donkey Cart Apparition, Las Truchas, New Mexico";

Superstition Review: "The Destroyer of Compassor";
Tinderbox Poetry Review: "In the Cottonwoods";
Vinyl Poetry: "Axis";
99 Poems online: "The War Museum";
1110: "The Riches."

A special thanks to Longhouse Publishers for publishing a pamphlet of "The Mud Angels, Mesilla, New Mexico" and "Crossing New Mexico with Weldon Kees."

"One El Paso, Two El Paso" appeared in *The Best American Poetry 2014* (Scribners), guest-edited by Terrance Hayes.

"The War Museum" appeared in *99 Poems for the 99 Percent*, edited by Dean Rader (99: The Press).

I would like to thank the University of Minnesota's Faculty Imagine Fund and its Scholar of the College Fellowship, along with The Vermont Studio Center, for support and space to complete many of these poems. Love and devotion to my wife Ida and our granddaughters, Jaedyn and Sophia. These pages were created with their voices and music inside me. I wrote many of these poems in the memory of my late friend, Morton Marcus, and my late teacher and mentor, Robert Burlingame. I dedicate this book to the two of them. With friendship and respect, I thank George Kalamaras, John Bradley, Phil Woods, Lawrence Welsh, and Juan Felipe Herrera. My gratitude to Peter Conners and everyone at BOA for their support of my work.

ABOUT THE AUTHOR

Ray Gonzalez is the author of fifteen books of poetry, including six from BOA Editions—*The Heat of Arrivals* (1997 PEN/Oakland Josephine Miles Book Award), *Cabato Sentora* (2000 Minnesota Book Award Finalist), *The Hawk Temple at Tierra Grande* (winner of a 2003 Minnesota Book Award for Poetry), *Consideration of the Guitar: New and Selected Poems* (2005), *Cool Auditor: Prose Poems* (2009), and *Beautiful Wall* (2015). The University of Arizona Press has published eight books, including *Turtle Pictures* (2000), a mixed-genre text, which received the 2001 Minnesota Book Award for Poetry. His poems have appeared in the 1999, 2000, 2003, and 2014 editions of *The Best American Poetry* (Scribners) and in *The Pushcart Prize: Best of the Small Presses 2000* (Pushcart Press).

Gonzalez is also the author of three collections of essays: *The Underground Heart: A Return to a Hidden Landscape* (Arizona, 2002), which received the 2003 Carr P. Collins / Texas Institute of Letters Award for Best Book of Nonfiction; *Memory Fever* (Arizona, 1999); and *Renaming the Earth: Personal Essays* (Arizona, 2008).

He has written two collections of short stories: *The Ghost of John Wayne* (Arizona, 2001, winner of a 2002 Western Heritage Award for Best Short Story and a 2002 Latino Heritage Award in Literature) and *Circling the Tortilla Dragon* (Creative Arts, 2002).

He is the editor of twelve anthologies, most recently *Sudden Fiction Latino: Short Short Stories from the U.S. and Latin America* (W. W. Norton). He has served as Poetry Editor of *The Bloomsbury Review* for thirty-five years and, in 1998, founded *LUNA*, a poetry journal, which received a Fund for Poetry grant for Excellence in Publishing.

He was awarded a 2015 Con Tinta Lifetime Achievement Award in Latino Literature and a 2002 Lifetime Achievement Award from the Southwest Border Regional Library Association. He is a Professor in the MFA Creative Writing Program at The University of Minnesota in Minneapolis.

BOA EDITIONS, LTD.
AMERICAN POETS CONTINUUM SERIES

No. 1   *The Fuhrer Bunker: A Cycle of Poems in Progress*
W. D. Snodgrass

No. 2   *She*
M. L. Rosenthal

No. 3   *Living With Distance*
Ralph J. Mills, Jr.

No. 4   *Not Just Any Death*
Michael Waters

No. 5   *That Was Then: New and Selected Poems*
Isabella Gardner

No. 6   *Things That Happen Where There Aren't Any People*
William Stafford

No. 7   *The Bridge of Change: Poems 1974–1980*
John Logan

No. 8   *Signatures*
Joseph Stroud

No. 9   *People Live Here: Selected Poems 1949–1983*
Louis Simpson

No. 10   *Yin*
Carolyn Kizer

No. 11   *Duhamel: Ideas of Order in Little Canada*
Bill Tremblay

No. 12   *Seeing It Was So*
Anthony Piccione

No. 13   *Hyam Plutzik: The Collected Poems*

No. 14   *Good Woman: Poems and a Memoir 1969–1980*
Lucille Clifton

No. 15   *Next: New Poems*
Lucille Clifton

No. 16   *Roxa: Voices of the Culver Family*
William B. Patrick

No. 17   *John Logan: The Collected Poems*

No. 18   *Isabella Gardner: The Collected Poems*

No. 19   *The Sunken Lightship*
Peter Makuck

No. 20   *The City in Which I Love You*
Li-Young Lee

No. 21   *Quilting: Poems 1987–1990*
Lucille Clifton

No. 22   *John Logan: The Collected Fiction*

No. 23   *Shenandoah and Other Verse Plays*
Delmore Schwartz

No. 24   *Nobody Lives on Arthur Godfrey Boulevard*
Gerald Costanzo

No. 25   *The Book of Names: New and Selected Poems*
Barton Sutter

No. 26   *Each in His Season*
W. D. Snodgrass

No. 27   *Wordworks: Poems Selected and New*
Richard Kostelanetz

No. 28   *What We Carry*
Dorianne Laux

No. 29   *Red Suitcase*
Naomi Shihab Nye

No. 30   *Song*
Brigit Pegeen Kelly

No. 31   *The Fuehrer Bunker: The Complete Cycle*
W. D. Snodgrass

No. 32   *For the Kingdom*
Anthony Piccione

No. 33   *The Quicken Tree*
Bill Knott

No. 34   *These Upraised Hands*
William B. Patrick

No. 35   *Crazy Horse in Stillness*
         William Heyen

No. 36   *Quick, Now, Always*
         Mark Irwin

No. 37   *I Have Tasted the Apple*
         Mary Crow

No. 38   *The Terrible Stories*
         Lucille Clifton

No. 39   *The Heat of Arrivals*
         Ray Gonzalez

No. 40   *Jimmy & Rita*
         Kim Addonizio

No. 41   *Green Ash, Red Maple, Black Gum*
         Michael Waters

No. 42   *Against Distance*
         Peter Makuck

No. 43   *The Night Path*
         Laurie Kutchins

No. 44   *Radiography*
         Bruce Bond

No. 45   *At My Ease: Uncollected Poems of the Fifties and Sixties*
         David Ignatow

No. 46   *Trillium*
         Richard Foerster

No. 47   *Fuel*
         Naomi Shihab Nye

No. 48   *Gratitude*
         Sam Hamill

No. 49   *Diana, Charles, & the Queen*
         William Heyen

No. 50   *Plus Shipping*
         Bob Hicok

No. 51   *Cabato Sentora*
         Ray Gonzalez

No. 52   *We Didn't Come Here for This*
         William B. Patrick

No. 53   *The Vandals*
         Alan Michael Parker

No. 54   *To Get Here*
         Wendy Mnookin

No. 55   *Living Is What I Wanted: Last Poems*
         David Ignatow

No. 56   *Dusty Angel*
         Michael Blumenthal

No. 57   *The Tiger Iris*
         Joan Swift

No. 58   *White City*
         Mark Irwin

No. 59   *Laugh at the End of the World: Collected Comic Poems 1969–1999*
         Bill Knott

No. 60   *Blessing the Boats: New and Selected Poems: 1988–2000*
         Lucille Clifton

No. 61   *Tell Me*
         Kim Addonizio

No. 62   *Smoke*
         Dorianne Laux

No. 63   *Parthenopi: New and Selected Poems*
         Michael Waters

No. 64   *Rancho Notorious*
         Richard Garcia

No. 65   *Jam*
         Joe-Anne McLaughlin

No. 66   *A. Poulin, Jr. Selected Poems*
         Edited, with an Introduction by Michael Waters

No. 67   *Small Gods of Grief*
         Laure-Anne Bosselaar

No. 68   *Book of My Nights*
         Li-Young Lee

No. 69   *Tulip Farms and Leper Colonies*
         Charles Harper Webb

No. 70   *Double Going*
         Richard Foerster

No. 71   *What He Took*
         Wendy Mnookin

No. 72   *The Hawk Temple at Tierra Grande*
         Ray Gonzalez

No. 73 *Mules of Love*
Ellen Bass

No. 74 *The Guests at the Gate*
Anthony Piccione

No. 75 *Dumb Luck*
Sam Hamill

No. 76 *Love Song with Motor Vehicles*
Alan Michael Parker

No. 77 *Life Watch*
Willis Barnstone

No. 78 *The Owner of the House: New
Collected Poems 1940–2001*
Louis Simpson

No. 79 *Is*
Wayne Dodd

No. 80 *Late*
Cecilia Woloch

No. 81 *Precipitates*
Debra Kang Dean

No. 82 *The Orchard*
Brigit Pegeen Kelly

No. 83 *Bright Hunger*
Mark Irwin

No. 84 *Desire Lines: New and Selected
Poems*
Lola Haskins

No. 85 *Curious Conduct*
Jeanne Marie Beaumont

No. 86 *Mercy*
Lucille Clifton

No. 87 *Model Homes*
Wayne Koestenbaum

No. 88 *Farewell to the Starlight in
Whiskey*
Barton Sutter

No. 89 *Angels for the Burning*
David Mura

No. 90 *The Rooster's Wife*
Russell Edson

No. 91 *American Children*
Jim Simmerman

No. 92 *Postcards from the Interior*
Wyn Cooper

No. 93 *You & Yours*
Naomi Shihab Nye

No. 94 *Consideration of the Guitar:
New and Selected Poems
1986–2005*
Ray Gonzalez

No. 95 *Off-Season in the Promised Land*
Peter Makuck

No. 96 *The Hoopoe's Crown*
Jacqueline Osherow

No. 97 *Not for Specialists:
New and Selected Poems*
W. D. Snodgrass

No. 98 *Splendor*
Steve Kronen

No. 99 *Woman Crossing a Field*
Deena Linett

No. 100 *The Burning of Troy*
Richard Foerster

No. 101 *Darling Vulgarity*
Michael Waters

No. 102 *The Persistence of Objects*
Richard Garcia

No. 103 *Slope of the Child Everlasting*
Laurie Kutchins

No. 104 *Broken Hallelujahs*
Sean Thomas Dougherty

No. 105 *Peeping Tom's Cabin:
Comic Verse 1928–2008*
X. J. Kennedy

No. 106 *Disclamor*
G.C. Waldrep

No. 107 *Encouragement for a Man
Falling to His Death*
Christopher Kennedy

No. 108 *Sleeping with Houdini*
Nin Andrews

No. 109 *Nomina*
Karen Volkman

No. 110 *The Fortieth Day*
Kazim Ali

No. 111 *Elephants & Butterflies*
Alan Michael Parker

No. 112 *Voices*
Lucille Clifton

No. 113 *The Moon Makes Its Own Plea*
Wendy Mnookin

No. 114 *The Heaven-Sent Leaf*
Katy Lederer

No. 115 *Struggling Times*
Louis Simpson

No. 116 *And*
Michael Blumenthal

No. 117 *Carpathia*
Cecilia Woloch

No. 118 *Seasons of Lotus, Seasons of Bone*
Matthew Shenoda

No. 119 *Sharp Stars*
Sharon Bryan

No. 120 *Cool Auditor*
Ray Gonzalez

No. 121 *Long Lens: New and Selected Poems*
Peter Makuck

No. 122 *Chaos Is the New Calm*
Wyn Cooper

No. 123 *Diwata*
Barbara Jane Reyes

No. 124 *Burning of the Three Fires*
Jeanne Marie Beaumont

No. 125 *Sasha Sings the Laundry on the Line*
Sean Thomas Dougherty

No. 126 *Your Father on the Train of Ghosts*
G.C. Waldrep and John Gallaher

No. 127 *Ennui Prophet*
Christopher Kennedy

No. 128 *Transfer*
Naomi Shihab Nye

No. 129 *Gospel Night*
Michael Waters

No. 130 *The Hands of Strangers: Poems from the Nursing Home*
Janice N. Harrington

No. 131 *Kingdom Animalia*
Aracelis Girmay

No. 132 *True Faith*
Ira Sadoff

No. 133 *The Reindeer Camps and Other Poems*
Barton Sutter

No. 134 *The Collected Poems of Lucille Clifton: 1965–2010*

No. 135 *To Keep Love Blurry*
Craig Morgan Teicher

No. 136 *Theophobia*
Bruce Beasley

No. 137 *Refuge*
Adrie Kusserow

No. 138 *The Book of Goodbyes*
Jillian Weise

No. 139 *Birth Marks*
Jim Daniels

No. 140 *No Need of Sympathy*
Fleda Brown

No. 141 *There's a Box in the Garage You Can Beat with a Stick*
Michael Teig

No. 142 *The Keys to the Jail*
Keetje Kuipers

No. 143 *All You Ask for Is Longing: New and Selected Poems 1994–2014*
Sean Thomas Dougherty

No. 144 *Copia*
Erika Meitner

No. 145 *The Chair: Prose Poems*
Richard Garcia

No. 146 *In a Landscape*
John Gallaher

No. 147 *Fanny Says*
Nickole Brown

No. 148 *Why God Is a Woman*
Nin Andrews

No. 149 *Testament*
G.C. Waldrep

No. 150 *I'm No Longer Troubled by the Extravagance*
Rick Bursky

No. 151 *Antidote for Night*
         Marsha de la O
No. 152 *Beautiful Wall*
         Ray Gonzalez

COLOPHON

BOA Editions, Ltd., a not-for-profit publisher of poetry and other literary works, fosters readership and appreciation of contemporary literature. By identifying, cultivating, and publishing both new and established poets and selecting authors of unique literary talent, BOA brings high-quality literature to the public. Support for this effort comes from the sale of its publications, grant funding, and private donations.

The publication of this book is made possible, in part,
by the special support of the following individuals:

Anonymous x 2
Nin Andrews
Gwen & Gary Conners
Wyn Cooper
Jonathan Everitt
Gouvernet Arts Fund
Michael Hall
Grant Holcomb
Jack & Gail Langerak
Peter & Phyllis Makuck
Richard Margolis & Sherry Phillips
Daniel M. Meyers,
in honor of Steve and Phyllis Russell & Grant Holcomb
Boo Poulin, *in honor of Daphne & Kevin Morrissey*
Deborah Ronnen & Sherman Levey
Steven O. Russell & Phyllis Rifkin-Russell
Michael Waters & Mihaela Moscaliuc